THE ILLUSTRATED
MOTORCAR LEGENDS

FERRARI

ROY BACON

Acknowledgements

The author and publishers wish to acknowledge all those who loaned material and photographs for this book. The bulk of the pictures came from the extensive archives of the National Motor Museum at Beaulieu, and we had kind assistance from the Maranello Concessionaires of Great Britain and Tozer Kemsley & Millbourn, who run their press office. Thanks to all who helped.

ISBN 1 85648 229 4
Printed and bound in China

CONTENTS

FOUNDATIONS

Ferrari road cars do not normally have cycle mudguards, but this 1947 Spyder Corsa 166 is a blend of the sports and racing cars.

Ferrari – blood red for Italy, as at home on the track as the road, adored by the *tifosii,* and the legend of Enzo. Cars, especially racing ones, are the third Italian male passion after women and wine, and Ferrari, the car carrying the prancing horse symbol, holds a unique place in their hearts.

Enzo Ferrari raced in the 1920s, ran the works Alfa Romeo team in the 1930s as *Scuderia-Ferrari,* and began building his own cars at Maranello to race in 1949. Many, many successes followed and Enzo saw his name come to represent the best in Italian exotic and competition cars before he died in 1988, aged 91. Road cars soon joined the racing ones: Ferrari built the chassis, but the bodies came from many of the famous Italian coachwork firms such as Carrozzeria Touring, Pinin Farina, Vignale, Ghia, Bertone and Scaglietti.

Production was very limited and many of the early cars were bodied to order so that most varied in detail or even on major points. Under the skin they all had the benefit of an advanced, strong specification and so were different from most new designs of that era. Commonly, these either adopted sophisticated but untried features that failed to work, or settled for the prosaic ones common to most makes.

Ferrari differed. From the start he realised the importance of a sound basic design so his engine, designed by Colombo, was a V-12 of 60-degree angle, with light-alloy for the block and cylinder heads, a single overhead camshaft for each cylinder bank, narrow valve angles, and hairpin valve springs. The first engine was of 1497cc with minute 125cc cylinders.

A fine 1949 coupe 166 showing the exciting Ferrari line that was there from the start.

Rear view of the 1949 166, the body by Carrozzeria Touring and marked Superleggera.

Interior of the 166, a right-hand drive model in which even the main instruments carry the Ferrari name.

Another 166 Corsa Spyder showing its racing car lines.

The elite specification did not stop there. Three twin-choke Weber carburettors (one on the tourers) and twin ignition distributors were fitted, the engine drove a five-speed gearbox and the chassis was tubular. There was independent front suspension, and massive but light drum brakes on all four wheels. This was truly exotic in 1947 and set the new marque on its path to become one of the most valued and respected while remaining strong, tough and very special.

The first 125 Sport became the 1995cc 166 Sport late in 1947, two cars being built, the first open and the second a coupe, both used in competition. Late in 1948 the 166 Mille Miglia with barchetta (little boat) body appeared for sports car racing, along with the 166 Inter that had a coupe body in most cases. Just three cars were built with cabriolet bodies having a folding soft top, while virtually all the cars varied in some way or another. The 166 Inter was built up to 1951 but this amounted to less than 40 cars in all.

A larger, 2341cc engine brought in the short-lived 195 Inter for 1951, around 25 being built with a variety of bodies by the leading Italian firms. Underneath, there was little change to the basic design and it remained exotic. While one carburettor, served by dual air filters, was the norm on the road cars, the triple, twin-choke Webers continued as an option.

The Tipo 125, such as this 1949 car, was raced by the works and some private owners in early postwar events.

The engine was bored out further to create the 2562cc 212 Inter during 1951, the cylinders now well over-square at 68 x 58.8mm, allowing the use of big valves and a high engine speed. Both coupe and cabriolet body styles continued to be offered by the established houses, some 80 examples being built up to 1953. During this time Pinin Farina began to supersede Vignale as the major force in the vanguard of Italian body styling.

While the Colombo engine had developed from 1.5- to 2.5-litres, Ferrari had changed horses for his Grand Prix cars, moving to the 4.5-litre unsupercharged type. To achieve the capacity required a longer V-12 engine and this was designed by Lampredi. It differed from most in having non-detachable cylinder heads, into which the cylinder liners screwed, which allowed the racing engines to run a high compression ratio to benefit from the alcohol fuel then in use.

From this work came the 340 America in 1951, its engine a massive 4101cc served by three Weber twin-choke carburettors and producing 220 bhp at 6,000 rpm. It drove a five-speed gearbox while the chassis followed the established Ferrari lines. Production was limited and most were built in a sports form with dry-sump lubrication to suit competition use. The touring cars had roadster, coupe or fastback bodies by Vignale, Ghia and Michelotti and most went to well-known people.

ABOVE: August, 1949, at Silverstone: Peter Whitehead's 125 Ferrari with the bonnet and camshaft covers off after its race.
BELOW: In 1950, Ghia built their only body for a Tipo 166 Inter, but used the same style for some later 195 and 212 cars.

Late in 1952 the 340 was superseded by the 342 America which retained the same engine but fitted a four-speed synchromesh gearbox. While the sports 340 developed into the Mexico and Mille Miglia forms for competition, the 342 was built for touring in Ferrari style. Only six were built, one having a cabriolet body by Vignale, the others bodied by Pinin Farina in cabriolet or coupe form. All were fast, comfortable and luxurious cars.

The final 342 had a larger 4522cc engine and it was this that was used to create the 375 America late in 1953. The extra capacity came from boring the Lampredi engine out further, while the power went up thanks to this and larger Webers. The sports version, the 375 MM or Mille Miglia, produced more power and the firm won at Le Mans in 1954, following the two Grand Prix titles taken by Alberto Ascari in 1952-53.

The barchetta, or little boat, body style displayed by a 166 Mille Miglia car from 1950.

Unveiled at the Paris show, the 375 America was accompanied by the 250 Europa. Intended for European customers, this was mechanically the same car except that the cylinder bore was reduced to equal the stroke which made the capacity 2963cc. Most of them had a Pinin Farina body, the others crafted by Vignale, both firms making at least one cabriolet. Around a dozen 375 America and 18 of the 250 Europa models were built in 1953-54 and these ended the early phase of the Ferrari road car.

Up to this point, production of the sports competition models, the Mille Miglia berlinetta type, exceeded the road ones but this was about to change. Enzo Ferrari was to move on, from building a few cars to help fund his racing, to true production, albeit on the limited scale expected of the exotic, exciting and expensive specialist.

The Lampredi engine made one final, later appearance, but the time had come for the return of the Colombo unit and the arrival of the 250 GT.

Not all Ferraris are red as shown by this 1950 Tipo 166 Inter.

ABOVE: A 166 Inter Roadster from 1950, with a cabriolet body by Pinin Farina.
BELOW: Similar style from Farina shown on a 166 Inter coupe, also built in 1950.

LEFT: Under the engine hatch of the 166 Inter lay the fabulous Colombo V-12 engine. This one managed on one Weber carburettor, but was fitted with twin air filters.

BELOW: The 195 Inter was only built for 1951. This one had a body by Vignale in a handsome, two-tone finish.

ABOVE: The 195 Superleggera came earlier – note the bonnet straps and extra lourves needed for track or circuit use.
BELOW: This is a 1950 Berlinetta 195, again demonstrating the variety of specifications that early cars were built to.

The 212 Cabriolet from 1951 had a larger engine. This one had the short-wheelbase chassis and a body by Michelotti & Vignale.

The fine 1951 Tipo 212 Superleggera with the open barchetta body giving it great lines and style.

The 'Thinwall Special', owned and raced by Tony Vandervell but originally a Formula 1 Ferrari, was powered by an unsupercharged, 4.5-litre, V-12 engine. Later came the Vanwall, but the Ferrari provided many valuable lessons and some good results.

For 1952-53 the world championship was run to Formula 2 rules and Alberto Ascari won most of the races, to take the titles using a 2-litre Tipo 500 car.

The Tipo 500 became the 625 of 2.5-litre for the 1954 Formula 1, but found the Mercedes-Benz opposition hard work.

ABOVE: Mexico version of the 340, built for competition and powered by the Lampredi V-12 engine.
BELOW: Open Mille Miglia 340 MM destined for track and circuit use although road-legal.

ABOVE: The 375 America was launched in 1953, this fine example is from 1954. It fitted the 4522cc Lampredi engine.
BELOW: Built late in 1954, this 375 America cabriolet was destined for Prince Leopold of Belgium and featured a 4.9-litre engine and a wonderful style.

Pure competition, a 375 Mille Miglia from 1953 displaying that Ferrari sports-racing style.

Years later at Brands Hatch, one of the many sports Ferraris fitted with the barchetta body that never dated.

FIRST LEGEND

October 1954 saw Ferrari unveil the 250 Granturismo at the Paris show. Listed as the 250 Europa GT, it was much more than a second series model as both the chassis and engine differed. Out went the Lampredi V-12, in went the 2953cc version of the Colombo V-12 engine, the capacity achieved by boring the cylinders out to 73mm while retaining the 58.8mm stroke first used in 1948.

The Colombo engine benefited from its continued competition use in the early-1950s, so was well developed for the new car and the series to evolve from it. It continued with its single overhead camshafts and three, twin-choke Webers, drove a four-speed gearbox via a twin-plate clutch, and was installed in a chassis of shorter wheelbase than the 375 and earlier 250.

Front suspension was independent by coil springs, while at the rear went a live axle riding on semi-elliptic springs and located by trailing arms. The chassis itself was a welded tubular ladder type, while the brakes were massive aluminium drums with iron liners. Borrani wire-spoked wheels on knock-on hubs were used – all very much the business for 1954.

Launched in 1954 as the 250 Granturismo at the Paris show, the type became the 250 GT Boano for 1956, named after the body builder. Later it changed to Ellena but this was the same firm.

From 1956, Ferrari offered the 250 GT Berlinetta 'Tour de France' for competition – this blue example is from 1959.

With one exception, the bodies were coupes by Pinin Farina and most were built in a standard form although there were detail differences on nearly all of them. Underneath the body, the mechanics were also built to a standard, even if there were still the variations possible in such specialist work. A number of cars had special bodies by Farina while one was by Vignale.

Competition cars continued to be built alongside the 'tourers', both for racing and as street-legal coupes and Spyders. They were listed as the 250 Mille Miglia or MM and the 375 MM. Meanwhile Farina often exercised his design skills to build a single car for show and public reaction. Some reflected foreign trends but most combined elements from the road models and the berlinetta style. Most were sleek, exciting and dramatic.

It was a period of expansion for Ferrari and Pinin Farina which resulted in more choice for 1956. It introduced bodies built by Boano that year, that company name changing to Ellena for 1958, but all produced by the same firm to a Farina design. The 250 GT added the body maker's name to its own, while the increase in production brought in quality improvements and fewer changes. Special bodies became rare for the road cars while single exercises ceased to be for clients and became evaluations.

The larger-capacity car was the 410 Superamerica, fitted with the 4963cc Lampredi engine, and limited in production. This one is from 1957.

Alongside the 250 GT Boano, Ferrari built the 250 GT Berlinetta 'Tour de France' as a customer competition car. Mechanically it was the same, but the body differed, being in aluminium; its windows were perspex, and it lacked most of the interior trim in order to reduce weight. More than one style appeared in the years up to 1959, the headlights sometimes faired in, while the final cars moved a small way from the stark competition model with a better interior trim.

ABOVE: Another 1957 Tipo 410 Superamerica which differs in detail as nearly all did. Most were built for the rich and famous.
BELOW: For 1959 the 410 Superamerica was in Series III form, having some mechanical changes.

The impressive 410 Superfast with a special Pinin Farina body in white and blue plus a number of special mechanical features.

Running in parallel from 1956 was the 410 Superamerica produced in Series I, II and III up to 1959. All used the Lampredi V-12 engine, enlarged to 4963cc, coupled to the four-speed synchromesh gearbox and installed in the long-wheelbase chassis. The result was, by Ferrari standards, a big and heavy car, but one well suited to the long American roads.

Production was limited, a dozen or less in each series, and most had Pinin Farina coupe bodies although Ghia, Boano and Scaglietti produced one coupe each. The Series II had the wheelbase reduced to that of the 250 GT while the III had engine, gearbox and brake improvements. Aside from the mechanical changes, and despite most having Farina bodies, no two cars were the same, reflecting the earlier, more specialist Ferrari days.

One 410 in particular recalled those times. It was built by Pinin Farina for the 1956 Paris show. Called the Superfast, it had a 4.9-litre engine having no less than 24 sparking plugs, the shorter chassis and a special body incorporating tail fins in the American vogue.

Two further models joined the range for 1957, but the 250 TR or Testa Rossa (red head) was a competition car, with all that implied as to increased power, reduced weight and special body. Its victories at Le Mans and elsewhere confirmed how strong and fast it was, and was the car to use up to 1961.

Testa Rossa or red head 250 TR was the Ferrari competition car to run in the late-1950s. This one is from 1958.

RIGHT: The Testa Rossa name came from
the finish of the cam-box covers, but the
six, twin-choke Webers made a greater
contribution to the power.

BELOW: Cockpit area of the 250 TR which
had the passenger seat as well trimmed as
the drivers.

The second model was the 250 GT Cabriolet Series I, the first true production convertible from Ferrari. Early examples varied, the first, used by team driver Peter Collins, had Dunlop disc brakes and the left-side door cut down in English style. However, most of the three dozen or so built had similar Pinin Farina bodies but with variation in headlight mounting, bumpers and side vents. All used the 2953cc Colombo V-12 engine and the four-speed gearbox, and the series ran to 1959.

A second convertible appeared in 1958, the 250 GT Spyder California based on the same mechanics but with the bodies built by Scaglietti to a Pinin Farina design. Unlike the touring Cabriolet, the Spyder was intended to be more sporting, so took features from the berlinettas to reduce weight by the use of aluminium doors and lids plus a simpler internal trim.

The Spyder was joined by the 250 GT PF Coupe, which had an understated style whose elegance lasted and was popular. Most of the mechanics remained the same but for 1960 the engine was revised to move the sparking plugs to the outside of the heads and individual inlet ports replaced siamesed ones. At the same time the clutch, gearbox and suspension were improved while disc brakes replaced the large, but sometimes temperamental drums. Production amounted to around 350, real numbers in Ferrari terms.

A 1959 example of the 250 GT Cabriolet which had the Colombo engine and a Pinin Farina body.

The 250 GT Spyder California had the body built by Scaglietti although the design came from Pinin Farina. This is a 1959 model.

In 1960 a short wheelbase version of the 250 GT Berlinetta joined the Tour de France model but remained a competition-oriented car, and a very successful one. One of the most handsome of the early Ferraris, the specification varied in many ways such as the fitment of the more powerful Testa Rossa engine, side vents, larger tanks and alternative body materials. Disc brakes were standard while the bodies were built by Scaglietti.

That same year saw the Series II 250 GT Cabriolet replace the earlier model, its appearance altered to distinguish it from the Spyder. At the same time the mechanics were improved in line with the rest of the range so there were disc brakes along with other items.

In 1960 Ferrari replaced the 410 by the 400 Superamerica Series I, a much changed car. In place of the Lampredi engine there was a 3967cc Colombo V-12, in essence still related to the first, but stretched out in both bore, stroke and power. It had all the advances added over the years such as outboard plugs and coil valve springs, but kept the short block length.

A four-speed plus overdrive gearbox was used but the chassis was as for the other models of the times. Disc brakes were fitted, as suited such a fast and heavy car, while all but two had Pinin Farina bodies, mostly coupes but with a few cabriolets. It was an expensive car, even by Ferrari standards, so production was limited to about four dozen, split equally between the short-wheelbase Series I, and the longer Series II built from late-1962 to early-1964. All were individual bodies so no two were alike.

More for competition, the 250 GT Berlinetta of 1960 which fitted the Testa Rossa engine and had a number of changes to suit circuit use.

Another example of the 250 GT Berlinetta, in this case from 1961 and not in the usual red.

During 1960 the 250 GT Spyder California was modified to a short-wheelbase form. It was, if anything, even better looking than the older version and also faster with improved handling. About 100 Spyders were built in all, split between the two lengths, and although presented as a competition road car, most were thought by their owners to be just too nice to race. Production ceased early in 1963.

The launch of the 250 GTE 2+2 as a 1961 model at the 1960 Paris show was, in some ways, more important. Ferrari and the body builder, now known as Pininfarina, had worked their magic to produce a Ferrari with four usable seats within the standard wheelbase. To do this the engine, a stock 2953cc Colombo unit, was moved forward enough to create some space and the four-speed plus overdrive gearbox installed.

The result retained the Ferrari style and proved a most successful production car, some 950 being built by late-1963. The forward engine and extra front weight bias had a marginal effect on the handling to increase the understeer but did not cause a problem.

In February 1962, the model that was to become possibly the most coveted Ferrari of all was unveiled at a press conference. It was the 250 GTO and over three years just 39 were produced and all are accounted for. Built as sports-racing cars, a Le Mans winner, and combining the V-12 engine with the five-speed gearbox, the GTO had a magnificent factory-designed coupe body from Scaglietti. Sleek, rugged and very, very quick, it combined all the attributes that made a Ferrari so special. They are now incredibly highly valued.

ABOVE: Series II version of the 250 GT Cabriolet for 1960 with the soft top raised.
BELOW: Soft top down and stored on this 1962 250 GT Cabriolet, showing its fine lines.

A 250 GT Spyder California from 1963, its last year of production. Here it is open with the soft top furled.

Late in 1962 the 250 GT Berlinetta Lusso coupe appeared to offer a luxury version of what was, in essence, a competition car. The engine was moved forward in the short-wheelbase chassis to allow more space in the body, it drove a four-speed gearbox and the rear axle was laterally located by a Watts linkage. The body was built by Scaglietti to a Pininfarina design and included true bucket seats and an instrument panel unique to the Lusso.

The Lusso was one of the most stylish of all Ferraris and by the end of 1964 some 350 had been produced, a fitting climax to the days of the 250 GT. In 1963 it was joined by the 330 LMB (Le Mans Berlinetta) of greater engine size which replaced the 250 GTO to be the last of the front-engined competition sports cars. A similar car was built as a 250 LMB.

Very late in 1963, Ferrari showed the 250 Le Mans at the Paris show to introduce the mid-engined concept on the road in a street-legal form. It used the 3.3-litre, V-12 engine, had fuel tanks on each side just ahead of the rear wheels, and a sleek coupe body. It was followed by the Berlinetta 250 LMB and the 330 LMB, but was usually coded as a 250 to aid homologation.

This is the earlier 250 GT Spyder California, from 1961.

ABOVE: This 1963 model was the first four-seater Ferrari coupe, the 250 GTE 2+2, with its body by Pininfarina.
BELOW: The 1961 250 GTE 2+2, a fine car in which four could travel in speed and comfort, as shown in the German brochure.

From 1958, Ferrari raced the Dino 246 and one carried Mike Hawthorn to the world title that year, the car remaining in use to 1960.

ABOVE: For sports car racing the Testa Rossa continued to be developed. This 250 TR is from 1960.

RIGHT: Most coveted of Ferraris, the 250 GTO was built for sports car racing from 1962 to 1964. All are now extremely valuable.

A 1962 Tipo 250 GTO showing off the fine lines of the Scaglietti body.

Special version of a 250 GTO fitted with a 4-litre engine, hence the front number plate on the bonnet.

RIGHT: Unusual 250 GTO Speciale of 1962 whose rear body has been amended to suit the tastes and needs of the owner.

OPPOSITE PAGE: A luxury version of the coupe came in 1962 as the 250 GT Berlinetta Lusso, a two-seater with very graceful lines.

BELOW: Rear view of the 250 GTO Speciale. The badge is marked 'Scuderia SSS Repubblica di Venezia'.

ABOVE: Another angle of a 250 GT Berlinetta Lusso, a great combination of speed and comfort.
BELOW: This 250 GTL Lusso is from 1964 and again emphasises the excellent line of the body which was built by Scaglietti.

ABOVE: Introduced late in 1963, the 250 LM Le Mans was the first mid-engined Ferrari coupe that was street-legal, although built for racing so hardly the most comfortable.
BELOW: On the 250 LM the body line was revised to enable the engine to be accommodated and scoops added to feed it air.

ABOVE: Rear view of the 250 LM which highlights the changed body line. Grills in the rear panels let the engine heat out.
BELOW: Racing 250 LM of the North American Racing Team, hence NART.

A 250 LM at a Prescott hill climb in 1968, ready to do its job well.

LARGER ENGINES

First of the new, enlarged cars was the 330 GT 2+2, introduced for 1964 and fitted with four headlights.

The 250 GT served Ferrari well for a decade, during which time he moved from limited, ad hoc, manufacture, to real, if still limited, production where the cars were built to a type, notionally all similar. There was always some variation, specials, competition cars and experiments, or prototypes used, adapted and then sometimes finally sold as a road car.

As 1964 opened, Ferrari began to change his model line and the first new car was the 330 GT 2+2. It retained the Colombo V-12 engine, opened up to 3967cc, while keeping the usual Ferrari chassis features but with the wheelbase stretched a little. Pininfarina provided the body which caused some talk for it was bulbous and had four headlights, the result having more interior space but less style. However, it reverted to two headlights in 1965 and proved popular, some 1,000 being sold over four seasons. The first 50 or so were known as the 330 America thanks to a badge on the rear panel.

Two months later, the replacement for the 400 Superamerica appeared as the 500 Superfast. It had an engine capacity of 4962cc, as for the Lampredi V-12 fitted to the 410, but was based on the Colombo design. The rest of the mechanics were much as for the 330 GT, both using the five-speed gearbox after a year or two. The Pininfarina body followed on from the 400 as a luxury coupe and the model was built in small numbers. Around 25 Series I were produced for 1964-65 and another 12 Series II during 1966.

ABOVE: By 1965 the 330 GT 2+2 had changed the line of the front end and reverted to twin lights.
BELOW: In 1964 the Superamerica became the 500 Superfast to continue the large-capacity, luxury theme.

The 500 Superfast as for 1965, a car for true Gran Turismo travelling.

Late in 1964 the 275 GTB berlinetta and 275 GTS Spyder models were launched at the Paris show to take Ferrari forward in both mechanics and style. The engine remained the faithful Colombo V-12, bored out to 3286cc and rated at 280 bhp for the coupe and 260 for the convertible, the first including the option of six Webers in its specification.

If the engine was simply an extension of an established theme, much else changed. The gearbox became a five-speed, synchromesh, all-indirect type built in unit with the differential in the rear axle, while independent rear suspension was adopted. The tubular chassis and front suspension remained typical Ferrari as did the disc brakes.

The berlinetta body was built by Scaglietti to a Pininfarina design and to some eyes suffered from its low window height. However, the 275 GTB represented the newer Ferrari style of high-speed, luxurious cars offering fast and comfortable all-day touring. Its success can be borne out by the 250 built in 1964-65 plus a further 200 as a Series II with body style changes for 1966.

The Spyder body was built by Pininfarina to offer a convertible model (later on hard tops were an option), and about 200 were built up to mid-1966. Along with the standard cars there were a limited number of 275 GTB/C competition cars built in 1966, some 12 in all. These had special engine internals, lightweight aluminium bodies, plastic side and rear windows, and larger wheels, all to improve their circuit performance.

ABOVE: Late-1964 brought the 275 GTB berlinetta which retained the Colombo V-12 engine, enlarged to 3286cc.
BELOW: By 1966, when this 275 GTB was built, they had become a Series II type with new wheels and other changes.

WJD 282S

ABOVE: The 275 GTS Spyder was launched alongside the berlinetta and had an open body and slightly less power.

OPPOSITE PAGE: Fine study of a 1966 Tipo 275 GTB which had its five-speed gearbox built in unit with the rear axle.

Early in 1966 Ferrari introduced the 330 GTC which combined the 3967cc V-12 engine of the 2+2 model with the 275 GTB chassis for the mechanics. The body was also an amalgamation, coming from the 400 front and 275 GTS rear, but the result was a most successful car. It was a pure Grand Tourer, fast and quiet, and used the five-speed, rear-mounted gearbox and all-round independent suspension. Some 600 of the 330 GTC were produced, and it was joined late in 1966 by the 330 GTS convertible of which around 100 were made. Both versions were built up to late-1968. The convertible fulfilled the same function as the coupe, although it was not as quiet due to the soft top.

In the middle of 1966 the range was joined by the 365 California, in a sense, a convertible version of the 500 Superfast fitted with the 4390cc version of the Colombo engine. The engine was directly coupled to the five-speed gearbox so only the front suspension was independent. The body was by Pininfarina, and production limited to just 14 cars, at one per month to mid-1967.

Another view of the 275 GTS with its soft top erected. The car shared most of its specifications with the berlinetta.

Late 1966 saw the appearance of the 275 GTB/4 which broke new ground for a Ferrari road car in having twin overhead camshafts for its Colombo V-12 engine. Fed by six Webers, it produced 300 bhp and the only visual difference from the 275 GTB lay in a slight bulge in the engine cover. It resulted in a well balanced car, very fast and well able to cover the ground at incredibly high averages, such as 121 mph for 46 miles south from Paris.

The 275 GTB/4 was built up to early 1968, around 280 being produced, while there was a NART Spyder version in 1967. This was special and instigated for the USA by importer Luigi Chinetti as a cabriolet. Less than ten were built at Maranello. The bodies were by Scaglietti and all were bought when they reached America.

At the Paris show in late 1967, Ferrari unveiled the 365 GT 2+2 which followed on the success of the earlier four-seater cars. It used the 4390cc single overhead camshaft engine, a true five-speed gearbox and independent suspension front and rear on coil springs, the rear self-levelling. Power steering and air conditioning were standard features and Pininfarina produced another fine body style fitted out with a luxurious interior. It was another success, production running to the start of 1971 and totalling some 800 cars.

ABOVE: A 275 GTB enjoying a day at Donington Park race circuit where its power and handling could be exploited.
BELOW: Another view of the fine lines of the 1966 Tipo 275 GTB.

RIGHT: During 1966 the 365 California appeared, in essence, a convertible derived from the 500 Superfast. Only fourteen were built.

BELOW: Front end view of the 365 California which was, for a Ferrari, large and heavy, but classed as a luxury model.

ABOVE: Late in 1966 Ferrari launched the 275 GTB/4 which saw the first use of twin overhead camshafts in a pure road car from the firm.
BELOW: Visually different due to the small bulge in the bonnet, the 275 GTB/4 was incredibly fast on the road.

ABOVE: A 275 GTB/4 fitted with a 'long nose' body but otherwise as the others.
BELOW: Late in 1967 at the Paris show, the 365 GT 2+2 was introduced. It offered the Ferrari enthusiast four seats, technical improvements and the comforts to create a family car.

Meanwhile, the competition cars continued the mid-engined theme. This one is from 1966 and is very similar to the 250 LM.

DINO AND FIAT

ABOVE: Forerunner of a new series, the 1966 Tipo 206 S which became the Dino Ferrari and had a mid-engine, transverse V-6 to power it.

While the Colombo V-12 engine continued in use in Ferrari cars well into the 1980s, there were moves afoot for alternatives. One such was to offer a small, and relatively inexpensive, alternative and work on this dated back to 1959.

Early efforts involved Fiat and several body firms, the results powered by a Ferrari engine but not carrying the marque name. Finally, the real prototype appeared at the 1965 Paris show as the Dino 206 GT Speciale. It had a 2-litre, V-6 engine with two overhead camshafts per cylinder bank. Dino was the nickname of Ferrari's son, who sadly had died in 1957. The engine went centrally, just ahead of the rear axle, and a very low Pininfarina body was fitted. The car was displayed on that firm's stand.

OPPOSITE PAGE: In time, the Dino V-6 engine was enlarged to create the 246 GT in 1969. This is a 1973 model. Neat treatment for the rear air inlets which were initially door handle wells.

Eventually, in 1968, the Dino 206 GT went into production. The 1987cc engine was installed transversely and retained the twin camshafts per bank. Production was by Fiat of Turin but the design was typical Ferrari who built a revised five-speed gearbox to suit the installation. There was independent suspension all round, disc brakes and a low, Scaglietti-built body which carried no Ferrari badges or insignia.

During 1969 the engine was bored out to 2419cc and the car became the Dino 246 GT while remaining beautifully balanced and a joy to drive on tight roads. Built up to 1973, there were nearly 2,500 of the 246, compared with just 150 of the 206. In 1972 the coupe was joined by the 246 GTS which had a removable centre section to the roof. It too sold well, running on into 1974, by which time over 1,200 had been built.

In 1969, Ferrari were taken over by giant Fiat. Fortunately it made little difference at Maranello where the marque kept its style and format.

Meanwhile, late in 1968, Ferrari introduced the 365 GTB/4 at the Paris show, although production did not commence until mid-1969. It took the 4390cc engine but added twin overhead camshafts to result in Ferrari's fastest and most expensive road car up to that time. It featured the rear-mounted, five-speed gearbox, independent suspension all round, and a coupe body built by Scaglietti. Known as the Daytona, it sold well, some 1,300 being built up to 1973. Alongside it came the 365 GTS/4 Spyder, a convertible with fine lines but built in small numbers. In fact, so small that some coupes were later converted by owners preferring an open car.

This is the Dino 246 GTS for 1973, shown with the centre roof section removed. The badge says 'Dino', and the car does not carry the Ferrari insignia.

In 1969, Ferrari added two more models using the 4390cc single-cam engine – the 365 GTC coupe and 365 GTS convertible which took over from the 330 series cars. Production only lasted for a year with under 200 coupes and a mere 20 Spyders being built.

In March 1971 a replacement for the 365 coupe appeared at the Geneva show as the 365 GTC/4, to bring the two-seater style back to the line. The engine was the 4390cc twin-cam as used in the Daytona but with a much-altered intake system. In place of the traditional bank of Webers in the vee there were a line of three twin-choke carburettors on the outside of each of the cam boxes. The inlet ports ran into the cam covers and down between the camshafts – this change reduced the engine height, and thus the body line, and freed the central vee for anti-pollution fittings.

The five-speed gearbox attached to the engine while the rest of the chassis was typical Ferrari and the smart body by Pininfarina. The model was intended to sell in the USA, hence the extra emission gear and some 500 were sold in a brief two-year production run.

Late in 1972 the 365 GT4 2+2 was introduced. It served to replace the single-cam version, which had left the range some 18 months earlier, but was based on the 365 GTC/4. Thus, it retained the 4390cc twin-cam engine, five speeds and other features while having a longer wheelbase to accommodate the extra seats in the Pininfarina body. It was produced for four years, up to late-1976, and over 500 were built.

ABOVE: This is a 1971 model of the 365 GTS Daytona Convertible of which few were built – a fast and expensive car.
BELOW: Following on the 330-series came models having larger engines, this is the 1968 Tipo 365 GTC coupe.

ABOVE: A 365 GTC from 1969 – the model was only listed for a year or two so production was limited.
BELOW: To replace the 365 GTC, Ferrari introduced this 365 GTC/4 coupe which had a good many changes and a very sleek line.

Further view of the short-lived 365 GTC/4 model, only built for 1971-72.

This Ferrari is said to be a GTB/4 Daytona Spyder so is most likely one of the coupes that had the top sliced off to make a convertible.

BOXER AND V-8

First of the Dino series fitted with a twin-cam, V-8 engine was the 308 GT4, this one is from 1977. The Bertone body seats four, its design a hard task.

Afurther version of the 365 series was first shown on the Pininfarina stand at the October 1971 Turin show. It reached production for the 1973 Paris show and featured a new engine type and body style to suit. The car was the 365 GT4 BB which had a flat-12, 4390cc boxer engine installed just ahead of the rear axle. The two banks of cylinders each had twin overhead camshafts and these were driven by toothed belts rather than the chains used in the V-12 engines. Four triple-choke Webers fed the mixture, the five-speed gearbox went beneath the engine and the differential was built in unit with them.

The body was mounted on a chassis built up from square and rectangular section steel tubes and had a rear-hinged deck to provide access to the mechanics. Designed by Pininfarina and built by Scaglietti, the result was a stylish car that handled well although less passenger and luggage space resulted. It was known as the Berlinetta Boxer, hence the BB in the code, and nearly 400 were built in its production run up to 1976.

Alongside the BB, Ferrari unveiled a second mid-engined car at the 1973 Paris show, the Dino 308 GT4 with yet another engine type. This was a Rocchi-designed, 90-degree V-8 of 2927cc which used the bore and stroke of the 4390cc V-12 and boxer engines. It had twin overhead camshafts on each cylinder bank, which were driven by toothed belts. Four twin-choke Webers supplied the mixture and the five-speed gearbox and differential were built in unit with the transversely-mounted engine.

The body of the new Dino was by Bertone who had taken on the tough job of fitting four seats in a 2.55-metre wheelbase which had the engine behind the rear seats. This he managed to do and the result was perhaps less stylish due to the constraints. For all that, the car worked well and had a production run up to early-1980, by when over 2,800 had been built.

This 308 GTS of 1978 was essentially a 308 GTB, but its roof panel could be removed to give open-air motoring.

Four seats and automatic transmission was not the perceived Ferrari style but came as the 400A. It evolved into this 400i Auto of 1981 which added fuel injection.

At the start of 1975 it was joined by the Dino 208 GT4 which was built using a smaller 1991cc engine to suit a 2-litre Italian tax threshold. Only sold in Italy, it duplicated the 308 in other respects and ran with it to early-1980 with 840 sold.

Before then, in October 1975, the 308 GTB joined the range to replace the Dino 246 GT. It retained the mid-engine theme using the 2927cc V-8 engine and other mechanics, but had them clothed by a Scaglietti built, Pininfarina designed, body which was mainly in fibreglass at first. In time Ferrari reverted to an all-metal body due to customer pressure. The popularity of the model was demonstrated by sales of nearly 2,900 before some major revisions for 1981. By September 1977 it was joined by the 308 GTS which was a convertible by virtue of a detachable roof panel and which sold over 3,200 up to late-1980 and revisions.

In October 1976 at the Paris show Ferrari astonished the motoring world by offering a model fitted with automatic transmission, the 400A. Based on the 365 GT4 2+2, it used the ever popular Colombo V-12 engine stretched to 4823cc, retained the twin overhead camshafts, the six Webers and the general Ferrari features. It kept the 2+2 Pininfarina body and marque style but the transmission came from General Motors and was their three-speed Turbo-Hydramatic. Traditional customers were quietened by the 400 GT which was introduced at the same time but came fitted with the five-speed gearbox. Production of both was modest and up to mid-1979 just over 350 automatics and under 150 manuals were built.

ABOVE: Alongside the automatic, Ferrari did offer the 400 GT with the stock five speeds. This is the 1977 model.
BELOW: From the earlier 365 GT4 BB, with its flat-12 boxer engine, came this 512 BB. This one is from 1981, the year fuel injection replaced the Weber carburettors.

For the 1980s Ferrari introduced this Mondial 8 which kept the rear-mounted, V-8 engine but stretched the car to improve the interior space.

During 1979 the models became the 400i Auto and 400i GT, the change in code indicating the adoption of Bosch fuel injection in place of the famous Webers. This kept the two models in production up to 1985 during which time another 870 automatics and 420 manuals were built.

October 1976 also saw the replacement for the boxer 365 in the shape of the 512 BB. This took the engine out to 4943cc but kept the general layout, style and Scaglietti-built body. While accommodation remained limited and the noise level high, the car continued to be one of the most satisfying to drive. Over 900 were built before a change to fuel injection during 1981, after which there were a further 1,000 before production ended late in 1984.

Late in 1980 production began of a new model, the Mondial 8 first seen earlier that year. It followed on from the 308 GT4 so kept the transverse V-8 engine in unit with the gearbox and rear axle, but had a little more wheelbase that enabled Pininfarina to provide adequate space for all four passengers. Fuel injection was used from the start and there were more interior creature comforts but initially it was not too popular, lacking the performance expected of a Ferrari. Thus, just under 500 were built by late-1982 when revisions came.

During 1980, fuel injection went on to the 308 series. This is the 308 GTBi coupe for 1982.

Late-1980 also saw fuel injection on the 308 GTB and 308 GTS which kept both going to late-1982 by which time nearly 500 coupes and over 1,700 convertibles had been built. At the same time the 208 GT4 was replaced by the 208 GTB and 208 GTS which kept their smaller engines but mirrored the body styles of the respective 308 cars. Both 208s sold well – the GTB over 1,700 to the end of 1982, and the GTS ran into early 1983 with 700 built.

The 208 showed its lower performance due to the 2-litre engine so in 1982 Ferrari added a turbocharger to create the 208 Turbo in GTB form which was an immediate success. During 1983 a GTS version was added and for 1986 the cars became the GTB Turbo and GTS Turbo, losing the 208 code.

The 308 GTSi continued the theme of producing a convertible model by making the roof panel detachable.

QUATTROVALVOLE

The 308 models and the Mondial both changed to four-valve, or quattrovalvole, cylinder heads in late-1982, resulting in more power and the 308 GTB 4v, 308 GTS 4v and Mondial 4v. This helped all of them along to the end of 1985, build numbers being around 750, 3040 and 1150 respectively. Late in 1983 the Mondial Cabriolet was added, offering an open four-seater with soft top, not seen from Ferrari for a decade, on the same mechanics. Over 600 were built up to 1985.

Four-valve cylinder heads were adopted by several models for 1983, as in this 308 GTB 4v.

The Mondial Cabriolet brought back open motoring for four late in 1983. This car is a later 3.2 version with a larger V-8 engine.

A rather special Ferrari appeared early in 1984, the 288 GTO which revived a revered code from two decades earlier. The intention was to build just 200 to homologate the car for racing but in the end there were 271. A measure of the hold the code initials had on Ferrari *aficionados* was that they sold without publicity by word of mouth, in fact demand was said to outstrip supply and markets were rationed.

The GTO was a fully-equipped road car which used the V-8 engine in a 2855cc form. This slightly-reduced capacity came from a smaller bore and was chosen to suit a class limit affected by the twin turbochargers fitted to the engine. Naturally there were twin overhead camshafts and four valves per cylinder, but the engine, while remaining behind the driver, was set longitudinal and not transverse. The five-speed gearbox and differential were built in unit with it, while the chassis followed Ferrari convention and the body was built by Scaglietti on a slightly-lengthened wheelbase. It was the first production Ferrari able to exceed 300 km/h.

The 288 GTO was a very special Ferrari, in a sense a return to older habits, for it was a road-legal racing car that bettered 300 km/h.

The 'red head' name was revived in 1985 when the Testarossa replaced the 512 BB. This is a 1987 model. The revised radiator position gave the car its dramatic style.

There were changes for 1985 when the 512 BB was replaced by a model known simply as the Testarossa. Meaning 'red head' in English, this was well remembered from the days of the 250 models of the late-1950s, but the new car differed in many ways. The engine remained a 4943cc flat-12 with twin overhead camshafts but they now opened four valves per cylinder while retaining the toothed-belt drive.

The chassis kept its expected features but the body, built by Pininfarina, evolved into a new style, in part to suit a new radiator location. For the 512 BB, it had been at the front, which required pipes to run alongside the seats, but the Testarossa had twin radiators, one on each side and behind the seats. Massive vents fed air to them and were protected by grills which gave the body a style. It was a spectacular car with a performance to match.

Early in the year the two 400 models stretched out to 4943cc by increasing the bore and became listed as the 412 GT and 412 Automatic. There were minor changes to the body but otherwise the models ran on to 1989. It was a time for engine enlargement, as late that year both the 308 models and the two Mondials changed to a 3186cc engine. The first pair became the 328 GTB and 328 GTS while remaining much as before in a form to continue to 1989. The Mondial remained available in coupe or convertible form, both of which proved popular and sold well up to mid-1989.

It was the middle of 1987 before the next new Ferrari made its entrance. This was the F40, produced to celebrate forty years of production with a model in the old style of a road-legal racing car. The engine was a 2936cc V-8 with twin overhead camshafts, four valves per cylinder and fuel injection plus twin turbochargers. It was set longitudinally behind the seats and produced 478 bhp at 7,000 rpm which went via a twin-plate clutch to a five-speed gearbox. It was not a car for the faint-hearted, as it was noisy, had a stiff clutch, lacked power steering or ABS, but was good for 200 mph. The body was in carbon composite materials, bonded to the tubular frame, and sported a massive rear spoiler.

In 1989 the 328 and Mondial models were further revised to fit the engine longitudinally and to stretch the V-8 out further to 3405cc. The first pair became listed as the 348 tb coupe and 348 ts convertible, the latter with a detachable roof section, both built by Scaglietti. Both had a transversely-mounted transmission, hence the 't' in the model code, and a body style featuring the side air vents of the Testarossa. For the Mondial t there were similar mechanics but a longer wheelbase to accommodate the 2+2 require-ments in both coupe and cabriolet bodies by Pininfarina.

The 412 model was based on the 400, so came in GT and Automatic forms, but had a larger engine. It was built from 1985 to 1989.

For the late 1980s the 308 series changed to a larger V-8 engine. This is the resulting 328 GTB for 1988.

At the start of 1992 the Testarossa was dropped, and replaced by the 512 TR which kept the 4963cc boxer engine now developing 428 bhp. It retained the twin camshafts and four valves per cylinder while the body shape continued but there were many changes under the skin of this new supercar. At the end of 1992 the F40 was dropped from the range, but its replacement did not appear until early in 1995.

Late in 1993 came the 456 GT to make a return to that first Ferrari concept of a V-12 engine at the front of the car. However, this engine was larger at 5474cc, had twin overhead camshafts opening four valves per cylinder and sent its 442 bhp into a six-speed gearbox. The body was a 2+2 coupe and the result was a remarkable car and a true Ferrari.

The Spyder model became the 328 GTS, such as this one from 1987 with the roof panel in place.

Same 328 GTS of 1987 in open form, minus the roof panel to provide fresh air to the occupants.

Mid-1994 brought the replacement for the 348 series but they continued on for one more year in GTB and GTS forms, to be joined by a convertible and the 348 GTC, a special edition limited to just 50 cars worldwide. The replacement was the F355 offered at first as a coupe, but with other body types promised later. It broke new ground for both engine and body although the mid-engine concept remained.

A 3496cc engine was used, but it had five valves per cylinder, three radially disposed inlets and two exhausts. Allied to a high compression ratio and all the Ferrari know-how, the result was 380 bhp at 8,250 rpm, the design allowing for future developments to a 10,000 rpm engine speed. A transverse, six-speed gearbox took the drive and had its own heat exchanger for a fast warm up.

The body was evolved by Pininfarina, working together with Maranello, to function with a chassis developed with aid from Niki Lauda, who had won world titles for Ferrari. The result was the use of ground effect, the low pressure under the flat underbody which counteracted the lift generated at high speed. Thus, Ferrari had a car able to run over 180 mph without the usual massive rear spoiler, just an upturned lip to the tail. There were also electronically controlled suspension dampers, power steering, ABS and a quality interior.

It was a remarkable car, far removed from that early 125 Sport, but one in the true Enzo spirit. So was Ferrari's return to the podium when Gerhard Berger won the 1994 German Grand Prix, for they had never given up trying. No-one could doubt that the F130 Barchetta, the F40 replacement, would carry the spirit of the prancing horse forward in 1995.

To celebrate 40 years of production Ferrari built the F40 for 1987, another road-legal racer for serious work.

Rear view of the F40 showing its massive rear spoiler, a feature needed in part due to the car's 200 mph potential.

ABOVE: For 1989 the 328 series had a further engine stretch which resulted in this 348 tb coupe.
BELOW: Matching the coupe was the 348 ts convertible, both cars adopting the side panel style of the Testarossa.

ABOVE: Fine brochure picture of the two 348 models which shows off their fine lines and style.
BELOW: Also from the brochure, the rear view of a 348 tb, the one most other drivers see of any Ferrari – and that not for long.

This is the V-8 engine fitted to both the 348 and Mondial cars. It features twin overhead camshafts opening four valves per cylinder and much other advanced technology.

ABOVE: The Mondial t appeared in 1989, its engine enlarged and the transmission mounted transversely, hence the letter 't' added to the name.

BELOW: In the same way the open version became the Mondial t Cabriolet.

ABOVE: Brochure picture of the two Mondial t models, Cabriolet at top, the coupe below.

BELOW: For 1992 this 512 TR replaced the Testarossa – it had many changes although it kept the body shape which was little altered.

ABOVE: Rear quarter of the 512 TR model showing its dramatic lines.

BELOW: For the 1993 456 GT Ferrari returned to the front mounted V-12 engine format of the past in a fine 2+2 coupe body.

During 1994 the F355 was introduced to carry on the Ferrari legend using the best of modern technology.

FERRARI MODELS

YEAR	CC	ENGINE	MODEL
1947	1497	V-12 ohc	125 Sport
1947-48	1995	V-12 ohc	166 Sport
1948	1995	V-12 ohc	166 Mille Miglia or MM
1948-51	1995	V-12 ohc	166 Inter
1951	2341	V-12 ohc	195 Inter
1951-53	2562	V-12 ohc	212 Inter
1951-52	4101	V-12 ohc	340 America
1951	4101	V-12 ohc	340 Mexico
1951	4101	V-12 ohc	340 Mille Miglia or MM
1952-53	4101	V-12 ohc	342 America
1953-55	4522	V-12 ohc	375 America
1953	4522	V-12 ohc	375 Mille Miglia or MM
1953-54	2953	V-12 ohc	250 Europa
1953-54	3300	V-12 ohc	250 Mille Miglia or MM
1954-55	2953	V-12 ohc	250 Europa GT
1956-57	2953	V-12 ohc	250 GT Boano
1956-59	2953	V-12 ohc	250 GT Berlinetta Tour de France
1957-59	2953	V-12 ohc	250 GT Cabriolet Series I
1957-61	2953	V-12 ohc	250 TR Testa Rossa
1958	2953	V-12 ohc	250 GT Ellena
1958-60	2953	V-12 ohc	250 GT Spyder California
1959-60	2953	V-12 ohc	250 GT PF Coupe
1960-62	2953	V-12 ohc	250 GT Berlinetta
1960-62	2953	V-12 ohc	250 GT Cabriolet II
1960-63	2953	V-12 ohc	250 GT Spyder California
1961-63	2953	V-12 ohc	250 GTE 2+2
1962-64	2953	V-12 ohc	250 GTO
1963-64	2953	V-12 ohc	250 GT Berlinetta Lusso
1964	2953	V-12 ohc	250 Le Mans or LM
1964	2953	V-12 ohc	250 Le Mans Berlinetta or LMB
1956-59	4963	V-12 ohc	410 Superamerica Series I, II & III
1960-62	3967	V-12 ohc	400 Superamerica Series I
1962-64	3967	V-12 ohc	400 Superamerica Series II
1964-66	4962	V-12 ohc	500 Superfast
1964-66	3286	V-12 ohc	275 GTB Berlinetta
1964-66	3286	V-12 ohc	275 GTS Spyder
1966	3286	V-12 ohc	275 GTB/C
1966-68	3286	V-12 ohc	275 GTB/4
1967	3286	V-12 ohc	275 GTS/4 NART Spyder
1963	3967	V-12 ohc	330 Le Mans Berlinetta or LMB
1964-67	3967	V-12 ohc	330 GT 2+2
1966-68	3967	V-12 ohc	330 GTC
1966-68	3967	V-12 ohc	330 GTS
1966-67	4390	V-12 ohc	365 California
1967-71	4390	V-12 ohc	365 GT 2+2

YEAR	CC	ENGINE	MODEL
1969	4390	V-12 ohc	365 GTC
1969	4390	V-12 ohc	365 GTS
1969-73	4390	V-12 dohc	365 GTB/4 Daytona
1969-73	4390	V-12 dohc	365 GTS/4
1971-72	4390	V-12 dohc	365 GTC/4
1972-76	4390	V-12 dohc	365 GT4 2+2
1973-76	4390	F-12 dohc	365 GT4 BB
1976-81	4943	F-12 dohc	512 BB
1981-84	4943	F-12 dohc	512i BB
1985-91	4943	F-12 dohc	Testarossa
1992-date	4943	V-12 dohc	512 TR
1976-79	4823	V-12 dohc	400 Automatic
1976-79	4823	V-12 dohc	400 GT
1979-85	4823	V-12 dohc	400i Automatic
1979-85	4823	V-12 dohc	400i GT
1985-89	4943	V-12 dohc	412 GT
1985-89	4943	V-12 dohc	412 Automatic
1968-69	1987	V-6 dohc	Dino 206 GT
1969-73	2419	V-6 dohc	Dino 246 GT
1972-74	2419	V-6 dohc	Dino 246 GTS
1973-80	2927	V-8 dohc	Dino 308 GT4
1975-80	2927	V-8 dohc	308 GTB
1977-80	2927	V-8 dohc	308 GTS
1981-82	2927	V-8 dohc	308 GTBi
1981-82	2927	V-8 dohc	308 GTSi
1982-85	2927	V-8 dohc	308 GTB 4v
1982-85	2927	V-8 dohc	308 GTS 4v
1985-89	3186	V-8 dohc	328 GTB
1985-89	3186	V-8 dohc	328 GTS
1989-95	3405	V-8 dohc	348 tb
1989-95	3405	V-8 dohc	348 ts
1994-95	3405	V-8 dohc	348 GTB
1994-95	3405	V-8 dohc	348 GTS
1994-95	3405	V-8 dohc	348 convertible
1994	3405	V-8 dohc	348 GTC
1975-80	1991	V-8 dohc	Dino 208 GT4
1980-82	1991	V-8 dohc	208 GTB
1980-83	1991	V-8 dohc	208 GTS
1982-85	1991	V-8 dohc	208 GTB Turbo
1983-85	1991	V-8 dohc	208 GTS Turbo
1986	1991	V-8 dohc	GTB Turbo
1986	1991	V-8 dohc	GTS Turbo
1980-82	2927	V-8 dohc	Mondial 8
1982-85	2927	V-8 dohc	Mondial 4v
1983-85	2927	V-8 dohc	Mondial Cabriolet
1985-89	3186	V-8 dohc	3.2 Mondial 4v
1985-89	3186	V-8 dohc	3.2 Mondial Cabriolet
1989-94	3405	V-8 dohc	Mondial t
1989-94	3405	V-8 dohc	Mondial t Cabriolet
1984-85	2855	V-8 dohc	288 GTO
1987-92	2936	V-8 dohc	F40
1993-date	5474	V-12 dohc	456 GT 2+2
1994-date	3496	V-8 dohc	F355